Lover's Credo

Also by Corliss Lamont:

Freedom of Choice Affirmed
Freedom Is As Freedom Does: Civil Liberties Today
The Illusion of Immortality
The Independent Mind
The Philosophy of Humanism
Man Answers Death: An Anthology of Poetry (Editor and Compiler)
Remembering John Masefield
The Thomas Lamonts in America (Editor and Contributor)

The sculpture reproduced above is one of a monumental series entitled "The Cycle of Life" at Oslo, by the Norwegian sculptor, Gustav Vigeland.

Courtesy David Finn

Lover's Credo

Corliss Lamont

With a Foreword by Bernard Grebanier

SOUTH BRUNSWICK AND NEW YORK:
A. S. BARNES AND COMPANY
LONDON: THOMAS YOSELOFF LTD

A. S. Barnes and Co., Inc.
Cranbury, New Jersey 08512

Thomas Yoseloff Ltd
108 New Bond Street
London W1Y OQX, England

Library of Congress Cataloging in Publication Data

Lamont, Corliss, 1902–
Lover's credo.

Poems.
I. Title.
PS3523.A4425L6 811'.5'4 74-39345
ISBN 0-498-01135-6

Printed in the United States of America

The sculpture reproduced on the front of the jacket cover is by Gustav Vigeland.

CONTENTS

FOREWORD

In these days when versifiers of no talent are capitalizing on the current wearisome aggregation of smut passing as the New Culture, it is a joy to come upon Corliss Lamont's *Lover's Credo,* where the holy sexual communion of man and woman in love is given its due. What I am most impressed with is Mr. Lamont's virile honesty, his unblushing apprehension of beauty, loveliness and spiritual sympathy that he can find in the beloved, his unstammering exultation of the sex-act between such a man and such a woman, and the incitements to such communion by the varying moods of untamed Nature herself. The two poems on skiing and sailing, by the way, are little masterpieces in their own right. Mr. Lamont's age is irrelevant; he has a heart that can never grow old.

BERNARD GREBANIER
Professor of English Literature Emeritus
Brooklyn College

PREFACE

Over the past few years I have become increasingly fed up with the cheap pornography, public nudity, and four-letter words that assail us from every side. The press is filled with advertisements of books on how to be supremely sensuous, and my mail is flooded with announcements of illustrated manuals on the innumerable techniques of the sex act. The theater and the motion picture vie with each other in offering as art salacious plots and scenes that throw to the winds any and all sense of sexual restraint. The movies literally stop at nothing. And as my friend Katharine Hepburn says, "Americans are becoming a nation of voyeurs." At this point I am terribly bored with it all.

I welcome much of the new freedom in sex that has resulted from modern methods of contraception and from the relaxation of puritanical restraints. But I believe that the sexual relation between male and female is being daily debased and treated as if the physical aspect, especially intercourse, were everything. The reaction against traditional sex ethics has gone too far, at least in the United States; the pendulum has swung from frustrating puritanism to pervasive obscenity and vulgarity. What I see and hear in the arts and media continually violates my standards of decency and affronts my sense of privacy.

What we need today in sex relations is more of a sense for the aesthetic, so that a keen awareness of beauty is constantly combined with a healthy eroticism and sexuality. That invincible combination in sex love has inspired many of the finest poems ever written, and much of the best painting and sculpture. *Eroto-aesthetic sensitivity*, then, is the key to the happiest and highest form of love.

In this book there are included reproductions of a sculpture by Auguste Rodin (1840–1917) and one by Gustav Vigeland (1869–1943). Of modern sculptors, I believe that Rodin and Vigeland give the most effective expression to the eroto-aesthetic relation between the sexes. Rodin's sculptures in marble of nude couples make the fusion of love and beauty come marvelously alive. Bernard Champigneulle says about Rodin: "With him passion is so exalted that it purifies the audacity of his lovers. The lovers seem to offer up a sort of pagan prayer which ennobles their physical attitudes. . . ."*

At Oslo, Vigeland's vast complex of nude figures, hundreds in number, illustrates the Cycle of Life and merges sexuality with the aesthetic in a massive display that ranks as one of the great artistic achievements of the twentieth century. One can spend hours of artistic appreciation and inspiration wandering leisurely through Vigeland's Sculpture Park, in essence a large outdoor museum that has no counterpart in scope and quality in the entire world.

I am publishing this sheaf of poems, originally written for family and friends, to celebrate the tenderness and beauty, the joy and passion, of love between a man and a woman. I try to make clear that love is likely to last only when the lovers share basic interests in addition to their

* *Rodin: His Sculpture, Drawings and Watercolors,* by Bernard Champignelle (New York: Harry N. Abrams, 1967).

feelings for each other. And in opposition to the cynics, misanthropes, and sophisticates of this era, I take my stand with the poets and affirm that enduring romantic love remains the greatest of experiences between man and woman.

C.L.

ACKNOWLEDGMENTS

I am most grateful to Bernard Grebanier, poet, critic, and Professor Emeritus of Poetry at Brooklyn College, for his advice and encouragement regarding *Lover's Credo.*

The photograph of Gustav Vigeland's sculpture, reproduced as frontispiece and on the jacket cover, is by David Finn and is used with his kind permission.

The photograph of Auguste Rodin's sculpture, "Eternal Springtime," is reproduced by the kind permission of the Metropolitan Museum of Art, Bequest of Isaac D. Fletcher, 1917.

The poem "Lover's Chant" was first published in *A Humanist Wedding Service* by Corliss Lamont (Buffalo: Prometheus Books, 1971). I thank Prometheus Books for permission to reprint.

The poem "Completion" was first published in *The Humanist,* which I thank for permission to reprint.

Lover's Credo

I

I believe in the creative and redeeming power of love between a man and a woman.

I believe in the uplifting of the spirit through the radiant wonder of loving and being loved.

I believe in the comradeship of shared ideals, in the gaiety of shared laughter, in the enjoyment together of Nature's beauty and man's unending genius.

I believe in the graceful rhythms of the dance, the swaying of bodies in perfect harmony, the magic of agile feet, and the dreamy drifting to slow music.

I believe in the companionship of outdoor life—in hiking, skiing, swimming, and enjoying sports together in the exhilaration of the open air.

I believe in the open fire's invitation to romance, with red flames dancing and logs crackling and two voices murmuring low.

I believe in the eyes of desire looking into the eyes of longing till the depths of one's being are stirred.

I believe in the dear delight of tender words—of *dearest, darling, belovéd, sweetheart, angel, my love.*

I believe in the witchery of summer nights and the thrill of holding each other close beneath the shining moon and stars in all their splendor.

And I believe in the frank and full-hearted celebration of sex love and of the exquisite sensitivity between male and female.

II

I believe in love as an unceasing fountain of tenderness, overflowing from inner springs of joy and growing more abundant with the giving.

I believe in the tranquil pleasure of hands holding hands—in every secret way—of fingers interlocked with fingers and gently moving.

I believe in the rapture of lips discovering lips, of the long deep kiss and of tongue touching tongue.

I believe in the loveliness of unclothed bodies and in the thrill—erotic and aesthetic—of looking upon my belovéd's naked beauty.

I believe in the warm, delicious feeling of physical togetherness and in the tingling joy of uninhibited explorations and caresses.

I believe in the wanderlust of unrestrained kisses and the freedom of gentle hands—lingering, encircling, straying—over breasts and legs and hair and the delicate, smooth skin.

I believe in the blessèd intimacy of flesh intertwined with flesh in every passionate way; the sense of oneness with my lover in and through every aspect of sexual communion.

I believe in the beauty of the ultimate embrace, the crescendo and ecstasy of fulfillment, the marvelous serenity after all passion spent.

I believe in the bliss of long and luscious nights of love, of dozing and sleeping warmed by each other until the late morning hours.

And I believe in love as a never-ending glory, as the creator of spiritual strength and as the joyous way in which men and women reproduce the race.

III

I believe in love as an antidote to loneliness and in the attainment of happiness through the constant sharing of experience with my belovèd.

I believe in the languorous ease of lying side by side on the soft and fragrant grass, looking up at the blue sky and watching clouds pass overhead.

I believe in the sudden glory of unpremeditated love—the yea-saying of the exuberant blood—in the hidden mossy nook or on the sandy beach with the sound of waves breaking.

I believe in the intimate whispers of unqualified trust and the exchange of confidences deep-treasured in the soul.

I believe in the escape of lovers from friends and family to some secluded Shangri-La to worship each other alone and at leisure.

I believe in the long and lingering farewell, with tender looks and affectionate words and the final reluctant parting.

I believe in the happy art of writing love-letters, in the indiscretion of the pen and the leaping wildness of uninhibited thought.

I believe in the simple delight of day-dreaming about my darling, of golden reverie about the heaven that was and will be.

I believe in ardent greetings after long absence, in devouring kisses and tears in the eye and the tight clasp of body to body.

And I believe in the purity and grace of complete, enduring love, in the exultant heart soaring free, in the flow of passion between lovers now and evermore.

Inlet and Tide

You are an inlet of the roaming sea
That winds among the many-colored rocks
And past the pleasant meadows green or tawny,
Your ever-cooling and alluring waters
Refreshing everything that feels or sees
The soft and shimmering texture of your being.
Now, with tide at ebb, your ledges lie
Bare and defenseless in the high sun's heat,
The fish marooned in lovely shallow pools,
And rivulets reduced to their last trickle.
Again you yearn for pulsing sea's return
And for the rhythms of the turning tide.
I am that ever-surging sea and tide,
Caressing you, possessing you, once more
In the wonderful ways of water flowing;
Into your every recess now I come,
The flooding sea, and swirl deliciously
Through narrow channels, rushing and rejoicing,
To rest at last in full tide's moving quiet,
The cycle done and consummation wrought.

Bay and Ocean

You are a bay, by rolling hills encircled,
Your tempting shores a tangle of verdant growth,
Your waves and whitecaps glistening in the sun.
I am the passionate, upsurging ocean
That daily freshens, replenishes, and sustains
Your beauteous being with far-ranging waters
From all the continents and seven seas.
Into and through you I in rapture flow,
Past your protecting islets, infiltrating
Through dark and sunless subterranean channels
Where wavy sea-weeds soft caress the currents.
O shining bay, you are my lovely bride;
And in our intimate intermingling
We fully, constantly possess each other,
By day, by night, in storm, in soothing calm,
Beneath the sun, beneath the starry sky,
And merge as one in Nature's harmony.

The Gift of Exaltation

Tender is the night always,
And tender every hour with you,
Under whatever sky; in all
Seasons, weathers, places, rooms-with-roses.

Swift is thought like light of day,
And swift the vivid thoughts that pass
Between us, glowing sparks illuming
The darkling labyrinth that is man's mind.

Life-giving the sun, and gracious-shining,
And likewise you, his truest daughter,
New beauty bringing to the world,
Raising banners of joy in human hearts.

Sweet the remembrance of fair women,
Lovely their faces and their forms;
Yet none so sweet in memory as you,
Deep-hidden, priceless treasure of the soul.

O slender stalk of budding flower,
O slim white birch so gently swaying,
O delicate spiral of fragrant smoke,
O golden, traceried leaf earth-dancing,

O grace in every mood and motion!
The sky-blue eyes so gay defying;
The autumn-auburned crown of hair,
The voice as if Beauty's self were speaking.

And we who've known your genius,
And the spell of your magic power,
Are so quickened in spirit and mind
We proudly walk transfigured then for life,

Feeling no evil can touch us now;
Fearing nothing in life or death;
Carrying within and down the years
The gift of exaltation you have given.

Palisades Memoir

I

Nature I can admire alone
In its many different moods;
But even more I hold it dear
When at my side walks one so fair

That she outrivals every flower,
Tree and creature of the forest,
Her radiant and her beauteous being
Lighting up dim copse and glen.

Gentle as she the June air stirred
When on that balmy afternoon
We gaily took possession of
The Palisades and all their beauty;

Treading leafed, pine-needled paths
And coming on those towering
Ramparts of long-crumbling cliff
Older than all our ancestors

Ten thousand generations back.
We looked, enchanted, far beneath,

Across the lush and swaying green,
To the river, wind-rippled white;

To the foaming wake of motorboats,
To slow barges of grey gravel,
To hawks and seagulls flying low
And floating on the fitful breeze.

Then for a single exquisite moment
The whole pulsating world was ours;
Ours to hold close, together,
As Time stopped at our bidding.

II

Hidden deep in wooded charms,
We found a rare and pleasant stream
Flowing between giant boulders,
And making muted, cooling music.

Down its rugged bed we went,
Leaping boldly rock to rock;
And once you came full in my arms
In all your maiden slenderness.

We reached at last the precipice
With its resounding waterfall,
Cascading out of sight to feed
The quiet, tempting pool below.

You were my dearest comrade then,
Sharing the dearest thing on earth:
The marvelous caressing warmth
That flows between a man and woman.

This was the absolute goodness
Of knowing absolute beauty—
Pure, innocent, and unalloyed,
With Nature smiling on our joy.

Let us be forever grateful
For that exultant day we dared;
For our youth, our health, our sex,
For the sweet merging of our lives;

For the long reach of the Palisades,
For trails and trees and cliffs and views,
For singing bird and sounding stream,
For Nature endlessly creating.

All Thou Dost Bring

Remembering
All thou dost bring,
I can but sing:

The eyes so blue,
The look so true,
The whole of you;

Thy form so fair,
Thy colors rare,
Thine auburn hair;

The lips blood red,
The jaunty tread,
The toss of head.

Thy step of grace
In every place
Doth beauty trace:

Upon a stair,
In open air,
In rocky lair.

Thy mind alert,
With ideas girt,
Is never curt;

No jealous pride
Or hate inside
With thee abide;

Sweet dignity,
Warm gaiety
Preside in thee;

In thy face shine
All virtues fine,
O dear love mine.

Conscience

So your conscience pricks you, does it?
Because on a joyous New Year's Eve,
An eve that will not be forgotten,
You looked into my eyes, and talked
Into my mind, and smiled into my heart,
And found there what I found in you,
Returning freely warmth for warmth;
You sensed new beauty being born
And felt that sparkling interchange
Of mind and spirit that presages
Complete and precious understanding—
Because of this, your wretched conscience,
Ye gods—your conscience—pricks! Alas!
Why do not *you*, the inner, truer you,
Prick the bloated bubble of your conscience?

On a Warm Day of Spring

Infant, now adult, always female, Prodigy,
Who had read all the Harvard Classics through
At the phenomenal age of 10.2,
Thus giving John Stuart Mill a run for his money,
Who read the *Greek* classics at eight, having learned the
language at three.

Prodigy who has disappeared to an unknown and probably
Prodigious island off the coast of Canada,
Where you are now basking—I hope—though, alas, clearly
not
With the sun-worshiper who issued the original invitation;
But Prodigy, why did you have to flee so far?
I could show you an island or two along the coast of Maine:
One with great big pink-white granite boulders
Bucking the pounding waves from a turbulent sea,
Splitting them into a hundred thousand fragments
Lit by the rays of the kaleidoscopic sun;
And then the quiet little sandy beaches, wind-protected
For swimming quite uncovered and unseen;
And faint, moss-cushioned paths through the silent interior;
And a sun setting behind blue hills across the restless bay;
Most exquisite perhaps of all, a finely silhouetted seagull
Gliding along air currents of the early evening

Balancing itself with still and outstretched wings—
Here are rhythms near perfection, uncreated by Man.

Or, coming nearer, do you know the much-neglected Palisades
Just across the good old Hudson—so accessible
To tired New Yorkers who have the sense to take their
weekends off,
And thus escape Manhattanitis and other dread maladies?
There's room for many a couple along the Palisades
And I know a place or three totally undiscovered by the
crowd:
One grassy glade at the very edge of a sheer and soaring cliff,
Where you look out over the river to faraway hills,
To cities and bridges and boats, and barges towed by tugs;
You see the steam spurt suddenly from a funnel
And hear the whistle an instant later, thus proving
Something that you learned in school was right.
And if you want, you can read or talk—talking perhaps
"Until thought's melody becomes too sweet for utterance."
It's pretty darned nice—on a warm day of spring.

"Eternal Springtime," a sculpture by Auguste Rodin
Courtesy Metropolitan Museum of Art

If You Decree This Death

I have loved you so long—it seems like all my life—
In sickness and in health, in absence and when near;
I have loved you with such devotion,
With an all-enduring fire in my heart;
I have loved you with such tenderness,
Wishing your happiness above all things;
I have loved you with such depth,
Seeing in you embodied whole philosophies
To which I swore allegiance before we ever met;
And I have loved you with such folly,
Risking for you far more than you can guess.

Can it be that such intensities
Will strike in you no answering spark;
Must burn themselves out in a bleak despair,
Flickering, thwarted, hopeless, dying miserably
Before a wall of cold and blank indifference?

If you decree this death, you will have killed
A beauty that had lifted you on high,
Brought joy and calm, and even ecstasy;
Deepening and broadening and straightening
The twisted, turbulent currents of your life.

If you will play the callous executioner,
You execute yourself as well as me.

Two Faces

Sometimes there is a look upon your face
So shallow, hard, and palpably expressive
Of vacillating versatility
And the veerings of a rudderless life,
I wonder if you've not forever lost
The gift of human sensitivity,
The admirable capacity to shine
In wingéd acts as well as spoken words.
Is not that tell-tale look upon your face
The reason why all men of depth and feeling
At last are driven to recoil from you
To find a simple human warmth and friendship
In women who are less complex and worldly,
No hard and shallow look unmasking them?

II

Sometimes, dear friend, you are so beautiful
That I in truth believe no other woman
Who treads this whirling earth can equal you.
Sometimes there is a look upon your face
So lovely, full of grace and dignity,
So radiant with living consecration

To the greatest cause and aim of all; and yet,
So touched with tragedy, as if you had
Seen and understood the sufferings
Of your own ill-starred time and every other—
Sometimes this look upon your face so moves me
When I see it that I wonder if
This is not the ultimate in beauty
That ardently I've searched for all my life.

Poem Incarnate

Some poetry is lived as well as written.
You were a poem incarnate, dancing grace
In that dazzling gray-green dress you wore!
And as I gazed upon you on that night
Past happy times came crowding to my mind
When we had laughed and gaily danced together
To spirited and most melodious music;
Free spirits were we for an evening bright,
Rid of the hectic fevers of the world.

Enchanting pretty were you on that night,
And happy was I in your presence sweet,
Bethinking back ten years or more before
To beauty earlier found and known with you—
Of tree and cliff and leaf-strewn, rustling path.
First in the quivering warmth of May and June,
Later amid the riotous autumn hues;
Ecstatic moments spent atop the cliff
Aroused in us a dreamlike mystic mood—
There flowed the sparkling Hudson way below,
Far-distant hills arising east and north,
And twinkling lights at eve across the river.
Then it communion almost holy seemed,
With you and all of Nature's glory shared.

Nothing can now disturb or touch all that,
Dislodge or move it from my memory;
Nor can the sometime follies, failures too,
That will beset the uneven course of love
Detract from the dear poetry of you,
Which still I warmly treasure in my mind
And oft recall in patient solitude.

Memories

Now it is full thirty, forty years,
And yet I can recall as yesterday
Our dancing, flirting, laughing, sailing, hiking,
With picnics on the beach or mountain top,
And watching sunsets with my arm around you;
Then we canoed in the caressing moonlight,
Dropping our paddles now and then to glide
Across the water smoothly, silently,
As we observed the fireflies in their flight,
Like tiny shooting stars that briefly sparkle;
And we would softly sing there in the night
Ben Jonson's old, immortal song of love,
"Drink to me only with thine eyes,"
And other melodies that matched our mood.

When now I let my mind roam wide and free,
So many dear, sweet memories of you
Come flooding back to give me secret pleasure
That's mixed with deep-felt pangs of sadness and regret,
But that's the way, we know, of life and love;
There is no happy life, but only short-lived
Hours or days or nights that may be happy.
As I grow old, I oft shall think of you
In those romantic, early years of youth,

And wish, like all our fellow human beings,
That we could somehow resurrect the past,
So I could cancel out my gross mistakes,
The worst of which was losing touch with you
And letting you drift subtly from my life,
When you and your good parents moved far West.

Alas, there is no magic alchemy
That can transmute a copper life to gold,
And change me to that other, better self,
The bright and joyful man I could have been,
Had I pursued you to the ends of earth
And brought our dawning love to consummation.

A Thousand Ways of Loveliness

All night I tossed and thought of you
In your thousand ways of loveliness:
You in your sky-blue bathing suit,
You, enchanted by the Saguaros
And taking photos everywhere;
You, making those little squeals
So pleasing always to the male;
You, a child again, gay-swinging
On a swing with carefree grace;
You, bestirred by people's faces
Catching in your camera
Children, Indians, and Chicanos.
These remain blest memories
Of our happy years of love.

Ski Romance

The night's fresh snow transformed the hills and vales
Into a white, fantastic fairyland;
And swirling flakes still falling veiled Mt. Snow,
Where resolute and eager skiers moved
In line, by twos, toward the double chairlift.
David, in brick-red jacket, pants of blue,
Was skiing alone and sharply called out "Single?"
To the pretty girl ahead, Elaine,
Who wore a dark green parka, yellow slacks.
"Yes!" she replied, and David jostled forward
To ski beside her in the advancing line.
They deftly mounted the two-seated lift,
And in five minutes were no longer strangers.
At the mountain's top they kept together
And chose to ski the big broad Snowdance hill,
Traversing rather leisurely at first
And stopping twice to view the lovely scene:
A vast, vague crazy-quilt of winter colors,
With white and green and brown all intermixed,
The snow and hoarfrost thick upon the trees;
Below, hard-frozen lakes or ponds, half-hidden,
And in the misty distance snow-clad ranges.

It was cold and fast, but turns came easy

In the new-fallen, dry powder snow;
They skied most everywhere, Elaine and Dave,
On that exciting mountain, turning, schussing,
Traversing, as they conquered joyously
The many delightful slopes and lengthy trails—
Like Deer Run—winding its way down through the woods;
Occasionally they left the open hills
To zigzag in and out among the trees,
Leaving behind their own tracks in the snow.
Their skill and gracefulness were almost equal,
Although Elaine had some slight edge in speed;
But in the diverse, dextrous arts of skiing
The two were excellently matched and knew it;
So both of them were inwardly delighted
That they by chance had suddenly discovered
An able partner in their favored sport.

Until the dusk shut down the lifts, they skied,
Then went inside the lodge to slowly sip
Hot chocolate, with cookies crisp and tasty.
They drove for drinks to nearby Encore Inn,
Where lone before a roaring, open fire
They sat back warm and drowsy and relaxed,
Their cheeks, from wind and cold, still red and glowing,
Their bodies toned to peak euphoria
From exercise in clean, pure, open air.
Tired they were—healthily fatigued
As they slowly drank their Martinis down
And chatted of their matchless skiing day
And how they would repeat it on the morrow;
They also spoke of other splendid hills
Each one had skied in winters of the past.

They went downstairs to sup and ordered promptly

Half a bottle of chilled Asti Spumante,
Toasted each other in the sparkling wine,
Toasted the Snowdance and the Sundance hills,
Exulted over "this great sport," and said
"A skiing weekend is the top of life."
Elaine and Dave conversed with animation
About the sports and movies they preferred,
About their colleges, their jobs, their pay,
The causes they supported and the towns
Where they had lived; and soon they realized
Their basic life-styles were quite similar.
After the meal was over they returned
To sit again before the pleasant fire,
And silently enjoyed the gracious heat
While holding hands, gay-smiling at each other,
And looking musingly and dreamily
At the burning logs and red-hot embers.

Elaine was stopping at the Andirons
While at old Encore Dave as usual stayed.
The night was clear and stars lit up the sky
As he drove Elaine to her sedan.
They stood a moment looking at the stars,
Both thrilled and awe-struck by the vast array;
Then as Elaine unlocked her snow-girt car,
They embraced full length, with merry hugs and kisses.
Dave said, "It would be very nice, Elaine,
To visit you awhile in your motel;
I'll follow after you to Andirons."
"But not tonight, Dave dear," she said, "not now.
Another time, perhaps, if that's our wish;
Goodbye, my comrade skier, till tomorrow."
Then down the road she sped, snow whirling behind.

Lover's Chant

Possess me forever
O sweet delirium!

Sweep through my restless blood
O delicious fever!

Intoxicate my mind
O surging madness!

Fill utterly my being
O mystic joy!

And spur me to great deeds
O soul's ferment!

The Ripple of Your Laugh

So often on this isle we love so well
I've heard the rippling music of your laugh,
Caught from your eyes the swift deep flash of wit;
Then parried thrusts from your gay, nimble mind,
And parted from you most unwillingly.
I would go home—O why did I go home?—
And think and think until my thoughts of you
Dissolved into the dreams of gracious sleep;
And always I heard the ripple of your laugh
Which has not sounded here for many a day.
I can see you now, see your blue eyes
And hold you closely (in the dance of course!),
But still I can *hear* you best—can hear
The echoing ripple of your happy laugh
And the laughing ripple of your voice.

A Sacred Shrine for Me

Wherever your precious feet have trod
Becomes a sacred shrine for me:
The well-worn streets of Cambridge town,
The walkways of the Harvard Yard—
Lined with their ancient, stately elms—
The grassy banks of the River Charles;
And your ancestral Tamworth haunts;
The laughing girl, the jaunty woman,
Hiking the springy woodland trails
To mountain tops more lovely made
By your presence, your shining beauty
Mingling with Nature's magnificence.
And I do cherish all other places
Where you have been or visited
And left the imprint of your grace
On the good earth and human hearts.

In Your Dark Days, Remember

In your dark days, remember, dearest friend,
That here is one whose love of you transcends
The deepest passions known by ardent men
Since first enraptured lovers sighed and stared
At beauty breathing in the form of woman.
When shadows fall across your life, my dear,
Do not forget the heaven we have shared
Or how our yearning bodies would respond
In perfect rhythms that entranced the soul,
And suffused our inmost selves with joy.
In your hard years to come, remember, darling,
That I am ever near to give you love,
To bring you back to life with my devotion,
To end our story
In climactic glory.

When I Was Alone

When I was alone at night
In strange and distant cities,
On trains which pierced the darkness,
I called aloud your name
I sang the song of your dear name.

Longing for your voice,
I heard your words like music
Coming out of nowhere,
Your sweet-sounding tongue,
Bringing me secret, sacred joy.

When angry, disturbing thoughts
Kept swirling through my mind
And would not let me sleep,
I remembered your auburn hair
And the little curl beside your ears.

When sudden pain assailed me,
And my soul cried for help,
I summoned up your image,
Thought upon your beauty
And drove the haunting demon out.

When I yearned for a woman's warmth,
I dreamt of your loveliness;
Felt your body's soft length,
Held close its tenderness . . .
Lovers' dreams sometimes come true.

Today I Weep

Today I weep, because it is October
And something gone never to come again.
That chance concatenation of events
Will never come again; that first sublime
Discovery that we were really one;
No, not if we should live a hundred years
Can that rich, unmatched, unmeasured moment
Repeat itself, to lift us to the heights.
For time, alas, is irreversible
And all defeats and victories are read
Into the unchanging and too often cruel
Immortality of the past.

There is but one September in each year,
Containing one last day and one last night;
For us there is a one-and-only youth,
A quickly passing one-and-only life
To relish the ripened fruits of all Septembers
And all the fragrant days and nights of beauty.
And so I weep for what we did not do,
For our retreat from shining glory when
We held it in our grasp; for our defeat,
Not by the hand of fate, but by ourselves,
Our strange passivity and unawareness
Of what our highest destinies deserved.

Next to Last Lines

(at 4:30 A.M.)

Do not think that I
Am too importunate!
To be away from you
Is for me a daily sort of dying.
And so I'm on the rocky edge,
Near death for forty days and nights,
Starved of your being
And thirsting for your beauty;
And though I know that you will wait,
A time could easily come
In the agony of separation
When this frail and yearning spirit,
Too passionate, too sensitive,
For the obstructions of space
And the cruelties of time,
Gives up the ghost to rest forever—
From love.

Do You Remember?

Do you remember still our all-day sail
And picnic on that limpid August day?
At ten we climbed aboard *El Jaleo*
And promptly hoisted sail for our adventure;
A lightish morning breeze filled the mainsail
As lazily the boat slipped down the harbor;
We glided through the hidden, narrow entrance
Dramatically guarded by an upthrust
Of boulders heaped on high by Nature's whim,
And looking like an ancient, rough-hewn pulpit;
A sea hawk's nest, where birds were circling, topped
The craggy pile, a sentinel well known
To mariners along the coast of Maine.
Out on the bay, as morning wind grew stronger,
We headed south and beat toward Crabtree Point;
We whipped along and cut a boiling swath
Of white-green foam, while iridescent spray
Blew fancy-free across the plunging bow,
And aft a foaming wake marked out our passage.

We fetched the headland in a single tack
And soon were sailing in more quiet waters,
Protected by that lovely maze of islands
Strung out for miles and miles in granite grandeur,

With sculptured harbors, inlets, cliffs and hills,
And shorelines—rugged, ragged, giant-strewn
With sprawling rocks of every shape and color,
Twisted tree-trunks, spars of old wrecked ships
And all the other jetsam of ten thousand
Ferocious storms and immemorial tides.
Do you remember, too, how then I steered
The boat within ten feet of that steep cliff
Where I, of course, well knew the depth of water
And where you had a faint access of nerves,
Then laughingly admired my nerve and skill?
Can you remember, as I do so well,
Everything we said and saw and did
That long, delicious day 'neath sun and sky?

At last we reached our goal of Outpost Island,
And on the leeward side dropped anchor safely;
We gaily rowed ashore and felt our way
Over the brownish seaweed-slippery rocks,
Then took the transverse trail across the island;
We sauntered through thick groves of evergreens—
All draped with beards of gray-green Spanish moss—
Enjoyed the forest fragrance and the shade,
Stood raptly listening to the massive silence
And picked up dry pine needles by the handful
To let them freely run through open fingers;
Then suddenly the path turned sharply west
And opened on a pink-white granite bluff
That jutted out above the surging breakers—
A height once shaped and carved by glacial drift,
And looking out in three diverse directions.

Do you remember how we sat and sighed
In awe that fused with wonder and delight,

Absorbing in a trance the sweeping view?
The mountain-studded mainland to the west
Reclining like a great gigantic lion;
The little archipelago engirding
The eastern sound; and then off to the south
Old ocean's lazy, undulating swell,
The sparkling glory of the restless sea.
We sat together on that beauteous bluff,
Held hands and talked, day-dreamed and reminisced,
Exploring deeply life's profoundest meaning
And our profoundest meaning for each other.

We rested after lunch, and read aloud
Some of our best-loved poems; then listened to
The white-winged seagulls cawing stridently
To their capricious mates in hide-and-seek.
We heard the wind a-gossip mid the trees,
The faint and steady splash-wash of the waves
Invisibly a-billowing and breaking;
We reveled in the mighty panorama
Extending in a broken arc before us;
In distant motion white sails brightly flashed,
While vagabonding clouds roamed o'er the sky;
The sun was summer-hot and warmed the rocks;
We felt its luscious heat and I remarked,
"The sun itself must worship you, my love."

Came finally the long sail home; we ran
With wind-taut sail before the stiff sou'wester,
Scudding past the myriad isles again,
Then racing across the choppy western bay;
The sun was sinking fast behind the backdrop
Of far-off mountains rising from the mist,
And soon lit up with opalescent glow

The long, low-lying strips of wispy clouds;
The breeze had lightened to a fairy's breath
As silently we crept into the harbor
And glided in and out the quiet fleet
Until we reached the safety of our mooring.
The day was over and the sail was ended,
But only just beginning was our love.

Faithful—to Our Past

Ever have I sought most faithfully
For beauty, warmth and quickness of the spirit.
It is the quickness one so seldom finds—
I mean a scintillating intellect
Fused with intense, inflammable emotion;
I mean a contagious sparkle in the eye,
A coruscating combustion in the brain;
I mean impetuosity in love,
And spontaneity that breaks through all
The cramping obstacles of space and time.

In you I saw this combination rare
And often dreamed that lasting love between us
Might reach the very summits of perfection,
Something unique, something of stunning beauty,
Yes, something that might even be deserving
The name of noble. So I've offered you
The highest that is in me and poured out
My heart to you with all the eloquence
That I can muster. Surely you now know
Whether you can return my love and share
The glowing vision that I have beheld.

But if you finally choose to close the gates

You must not ever think that I'll regret
Any moment I have spent with you,
Or ever say it was all waste and folly.
These feelings have been felt, these words were spoken;
Those hours lived are now a part of me;
The splendor of them will not soon be dimmed.
I shall be always faithful to our past
And to my blessèd memories of you;
There can be no regrets, but only wonder,
And gratitude, that we as humankind
Are so exquisitely compacted that
You and I could share such happiness.

Deep in My Blood

How forcefully you stir within my blood!
And now I know that you will ever be
Deep in my blood—that precious balm of life
Which gives me strength to love and worship you,
And flows to heart, to hands, to limbs, to lips,
To every dear and secret place of passion.
My God, it's sweet to be in love with you
And feel that you are rampant in my veins.
And I am glad that you are thus a part
Of me, behind and in and running through
My every thought and act, an indwelling,
Electrifying force that penetrates
The core and inmost essence of my being,
An utter, final taking hold of me.

Something Very Precious

I have something very precious, friend,
Something whose worth can never fluctuate,
Something that ever will stand me in good stead
In all the many crises of my life,
And even in my daily humdrum ways;
Something that strengthens, that makes light the task,
Releases all my hidden energies,
And fills my mind with boundless thoughts of beauty;
Something inspiring me to better work,
Since you, perchance, will judge the worth of it
And say perhaps, "Yes, this is rather good."
So you can see the value of my treasure;
I mean, my dear, the love you give to me.

Beyond All Words

I've read the greatest novels of love
And all the greatest poems of love,
As well as the major works of Freud,
His chief disciples and Alfred Kinsey;
And I have talked to psychiatrists,
To psychoanalysts galore,
To married and unmarried lovers
Both young and old, both woman and man;
But I have never seen or heard
Any depiction of love that even
Approaches what I feel for you.

I've tried to say all this in letters,
On walks, on lengthy airplane flights
O'er land and sea; when getting high
On Martinis or on Bloody Marys,
And during secluded tête-à-têtes;
But I am never more successful
Than Shakespeare, Milton, Shelley, Keats.
So now I know that my great passion
Truly is beyond all words—
Indeed ineffable—save when
I speak to you with my whole being
In the sweetness and the rapture,
And the rhythm of lovely love.

To the Lady of the Portrait

Behold a face of striking beauty
That deeply moves all manner of men,
Most of all this saddened swain
Who loved it and was sent by it
Wandering down the length of years
Unwept, unhonored—and unstrung!
I thank the painter of this portrait
Whose art so perfectly abstracts
The ideal essence of my love.
Here is the verve, the strength, the quick
All-sensing wit, the emerging mind,
The all-but-suppressed crusading spirit
Faintly refulgent nonetheless.
This face, too, has mystic power
That sweeps away with cleansing force
The shallowness of Platonic posing
And tells me in an age-long language
That once I love, I love forever.

This face is one that could make history,
Whose brow could pierce beneath the surface
Of life, and its central issues grasp.
You won't fulfill your life's high hope
Until you commit yourself, your dreams,
Your genius to a something greater

Than "What I've always longed to do,"
Though what a person longs to do
Can easily fit the higher aims,
Creating art that will endure.

The Greeks had gods and city-states,
The West its Christianity,
But what, dear madam, do you have?
Well, I ask you to consider
This era's most hopeful, vital movement:
The Humanistic way of life,
Mature in wisdom, young in spirit,
Inspiring men to noble deeds,
Deflecting from stale, stagnant waters
The swift, broad currents of human living,
Welding the weak, the strong, the wayward
From every land and every calling
Into a consecrated force.

Give Me the Strength

Give me but the strength, my ever dearest,
To follow the vision I have seen with you—
The radiant dream of love complete and lasting:
A man and woman perfectly attuned,
So every impulse of their souls and bodies
Awakes response and mutual understanding;
Who share, as well, the view that life can be
A constant wonder, joy and wild desire,
Commixed with a prevailing gaiety
And jaunty triumph over every ill;

Two lovers in whom the sense of beauty, too,
Is much akin, and whose ideals and aims
Amid the conflicting currents of our time,
And in the great causes, battles, strivings
For freedom, justice, peace—are quite the same.
Give me the strength, belovéd, to dismiss
Old habits and the fear of mental turmoil,
To come to you, fulfill love's ardent dream
And make our pulsing lives an endless song,
A masterpiece of meaning and creation.

Testament

Whatever I do, whatever I write or say,
Always know this: that I'm in love with you,
And *will* love you as long as I remain
A living man. That which is between us
Cannot be broken. I have tried to break it,
But it's a thousand times beyond my strength.
I've roundly cursed you, hated you and damned you
Because of your brusque and brutal thoughtlessness,
Sometimes for things outside of your control.
True, I have been rash, wild, foolish, fitful,
But think you what it is that's made me so:
You know about the pangs of frustrate passion,
How seethes and pounds and surges the hot blood;
You know beyond all doubt what true love is,
And that I, your lover, am in love with you.

Completion

No joy, no beauty, no adventure
For me can be complete and rounded
Till I've recounted it to you;
Till I have seen your eyes light up,
Your smile reach to the story's essence;
Until I've heard your searching comment
Or sensed from the look upon your face
Appreciation or genial scorn.
Only then can anything
For me be finished or assessed.
As with events from day to day,
So with my life from year to year;
Without you it is incomplete,
A heart-ache and a dismal waste.
Do you see, now, what love can mean?

Creation

They talk about the creative genius
Of artists, authors, scientists and statesmen;
But you and I together, belovéd,
A man and woman average in talent,
Possess the precious power to create,
Through our ennobling love for one another,
An actual human being, a baby,
Who then will grow, mature, become an adult
And full-fledged member of the human race
With infinite potentialities
For happiness, achievement, service to man.
This gift sublime of creativity,
Bestowed by Nature on all living things,
Expands, enriches love's essential meaning,
Makes everyone in love a kind of god,
And blesses human sexuality
As the wonderful and happy way
To guarantee a future for mankind.

Victory

To you, my sweet, I am forever grateful
For many new-found beauties in my life.
You blithely turn the present into rapture
And make the future promise sheerest joy.
Even my bitter past you have redeemed,
Bestowing on it new significance.
It is the end that counts and gives to all
That went before its full and final meaning,
Transforming the defeats, humiliations,
Dead-end sorties, insane infatuations,
To merest incidents in my long search,
Or lessons fraught with wisdom for the heart,
Or stepping stones to our great victory
Of happy love and lasting comradeship.

For you, beloved, I am forever grateful.
For [illegible] beautified our life.
Let [illegible] the [illegible] into [illegible]
And [illegible] we [illegible] joy.
[illegible]
De[illegible]
It is [illegible] and [illegible] to all
That we, together, [illegible] and [illegible] meaning.
Transforming the [illegible] boundaries.
Deal[illegible] infinitude.
To [illegible] long search
Of [illegible] wisdom for the heart.
[illegible] great victory
[illegible] love and lasting comradeship.